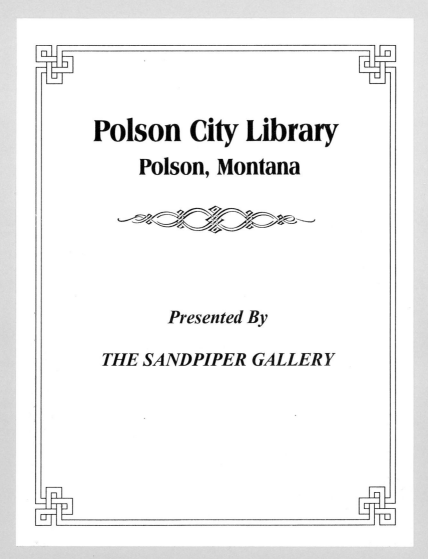

How Artists Use

Shape

Paul Flux

Heinemann Library
Chicago, Illinois

Designed by Celia Floyd
Illustrations by Jo Brooker/Ann Miller
Originated by Ambassador Litho Ltd.
Printed and bound in Hong Kong/China

05 04 03 02 01
10 9 8 7 6 5 4 3 2

Library of Congress Cataloging-in-Publication Data
Flux, Paul, 1952-
    Shape / Paul Flux.
      p. cm.--(How artists use)
    Includes bibliographical references (p.) and index.
    ISBN 1-58810-081-2 (lib. bdg.)
    1. Geometry in art--Juvenile literature. 2. Art--Technique--Juvenile literature. [1.
  Geometry in art. 2. Art--Technique.] I. Title.

N8217.G44 F58 2001
701'.8--dc21
                                                    00-058149

Acknowledgments
The Publishers would like to thank the following for permission to reproduce photographs:

AKG, London, pp. 10, 20; © ADAGP, Paris and DACS, London, 2001, p. 15; Eric Lessing Museo Nazionale Naples, p. 9; © DACS 2001, p. 11; National Gallery of Ireland, p. 19; Art Archive/Tate Gallery, London/© Succession Picasso/DACS 2001, p. 21; Bridgeman Art Library/© ADAGP, Paris and DACS, London, 2001, p. 5; Bolton Museum and Art Gallery, Lancashire/©Angela Verren-Taunt, 2001. All Rights Reserved, DACS, p. 18, Duke of Sutherland Collection/National Gallery of Scotland, p. 12; St. Peter's, Vatican, Rome, p. 17; Corbis/Philadelphia Museum of Art, pp. 13, 14; Giaraudon, p. 7; Henry Moore Foundation, p16; Hermitage, St Petersburg/© ADAGP, Paris and DACS, London 2001, p. 24; M. C. Escher's *Fishes and Scales* ©2000 Cordon Art B.V.-Baarn-Holland, p.8; National Gallery, Scotland/Estate of S. J. Peploe, p. 26; Tate Gallery, p. 4; Trevor Clifford, pp. 28, 29.

Cover photograph reproduced with permission of Bridgeman Art Library.

Every effort has been made to contact copyright holders of any material reproduced in this book. Any omissions will be rectified in subsequent printings if notice is given to the Publisher.

Some words are in bold, **like this.** You can find
out what they mean by looking in the glossary.

Contents

What Is Shape?

How many different shapes can you see in this picture? The title suggests we are looking at a room, perhaps the place where the artist works. Some of the squares may be paintings stacked against the wall. Our world is full of shapes: squares, circles, triangles—even some that have no names. Some artists arrange shapes so that we can recognize objects in their paintings. Others use shape to make **abstract** pictures.

Wyndham Lewis,
Workshop,
1914–1915

4

Wassily Kandinsky, *Intersecting Lines*, 1923

One way of thinking about a shape is to see it as an
outline that is filled in with color. This picture is full of
different shapes. How many can you see? Start at
the bottom right-hand corner and look toward the top
left-hand corner. The dark line that crosses the painting
makes the shapes appear to be flying away from you.

Common Shapes

Shapes are everywhere! An artist draws a line, joins it with other lines, and fills in the space with color. A shape is made. Shapes cannot exist on their own; the space around them makes other shapes. A picture is a collection of shapes that fit together, like a jigsaw puzzle. Artists can use shape to make us look at a picture in a particular way.

6

Leonardo da Vinci,
Mona Lisa, 1503

This is one of the most famous paintings in the world. It is by the Italian artist Leonardo da Vinci. The eyes of the woman seem to follow you when you move around. The **triangular** shape of her head and body lead your eyes upward. This is why you are always drawn back to look at her face.

7

M. C. Escher,
Fish and Scales,
1959

Shapes affect the space around them. In this picture you first notice the lines of white fish. But look at the space between them. In the middle are two sets of fish scales. As your eyes follow them they change into small fish that get bigger. No space is wasted. Everywhere you look, you see fish.

This is a **mosaic**, a picture made from hundreds of small pieces of colored glass and **marble**. It was made more than 2,000 years ago. The artist showed all the fish and sea creatures that lived in the water near the old city of Pompeii, Italy. The fish are shown in action. Their bodies are curved as if they are swimming.

Roman mosaic, Pompeii, Italy

Colored Shapes

This is one of the earliest paintings ever made. It was painted around 17,000 years ago! The horse was drawn with a single line. The **outline** was then colored in with an unusual **shade** of yellow. Around the young horse are shapes that look like grass, insects, and even birds. Although this picture was painted long ago, the artist skillfully showed the movement of a real animal.

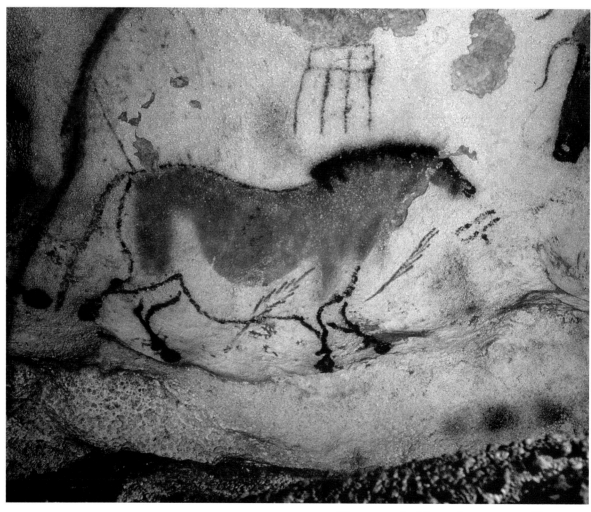

Cave painting, Lascaux, France

Franz Marc, *The Yellow Cow*, 1911

Here is an animal set in an imaginary **landscape** of colorful shapes. Even though the mountains are little more than triangles in the background, you know they are mountains. The same can be said for the trees and the grass around the cow. The colors and shapes in this painting, such as the upwardly curving line of the cow's neck, make the cow seem happy.

Shape and Portraits

Rembrandt van Rijn,
Self-Portrait,
aged 51, about 1657

In this **portrait** you see the **solid** shape of the artist looking straight back at you. He looks worried, almost sad. The dark shadows **emphasize** the shape of an unhappy man. Rembrandt painted many portraits of himself. When he was young he showed himself happy and successful. But toward the end of his life, when he was poor, he painted himself like this.

Here the artist has exaggerated shapes to create an unusual effect. The woman's neck and her small head seem carefully balanced. They contrast with the heavy, solid shape of her dark dress. Like the *Mona Lisa* on page 7, the **triangular** shape of the figure leads your eyes to the top of the picture, to the woman's head.

Amedeo Modigliani,
Portrait of a Polish Woman,
1919

Shape and Landscapes

In this picture you see houses bathed in sunlight. None of the shapes is very clear. Even though the roofs blend into the green trees, the picture shows a **landscape** that you recognize as being a real place.

Paul Cézanne, *Mont Sainte-Victoire,* **1902–1906**

Georges Braque, *Houses at L'Estaque,* 1908

Here is a similar **scene.** The buildings are **solid** shapes broken up by light and shadow. Instead of blurring the shapes, the artist has focused on using basic shapes, or cubes, to show houses. This use of basic shapes is called **Cubism.** This painting also shows houses blending in with the landscape around them.

Shapes and Sculpture

Henry Moore, *Sheep Piece*, 1971–1972

This **sculpture** was made in **bronze** so that it would not fade or rust. The soft lines of the sculpture are like the soft lines of real sheep. The artist has used shape to show the living form of animals. The sculpture is meant to be a part of the real-life **landscape**.

Michelangelo,
*Pietà,*1498–1499

Look at the folds of cloth and the way the bodies seem to come to life in this sculpture. It does not look like it is made of **marble,** a very hard rock. The artist has cut the marble into smooth, curving lines so the cloth looks like it is lightly draped around the people.

Shapes to Make Us Think

This peaceful **landscape** is made of colored shapes, each pushing against its neighbor. Do you think this looks like a real **scene?** If the houses, trees, and sky were missing it might look like an **abstract** painting.

Ben Nicholson, *Cornish Landscape,* **1940**

Here, light floods in through a window as one woman looks outside and another writes at her desk. Although there is a lot of light in the picture, the space seems enclosed by strong shapes. There are many sharp angles such as the corners of the window and the floor tile. The people, however, are painted with rounded lines.

Shapes and Feeling

Kasimir Malevich, *Suprematism,* 1915

The artist did not try to show real-life objects in this painting. Instead, the shapes and colors alone create a picture. The artist chose to use only straight, bold shapes. If these shapes were curved instead of straight, the painting would probably make you think of something very different than it does now.

Pablo Picasso painted this picture when he was angry about the Spanish Civil War. The woman's head is a strange shape because the **grief** she is feeling has changed what she looks like. The straight lines of the background **contrast** with the twisted shapes of her face to create a painting full of **emotion.**

Shape Outlines

Do you recognize these shapes? Without **shade** and **detail** some shapes can be confusing and difficult to recognize, while others are very easy. Try drawing some **outlines** of objects yourself, or copy some of these. Fill them in with details that make the shapes recognizable.

Choose an animal and make an outline of it. Copy one from page 22 if you like. Draw another two outlines of the same animal in different positions. Cut the three shapes out, and arrange them on a piece of paper. Trace around them, then add some details and color the spaces between the shapes. Try using different colors until you have a picture you like.

23

Making a Picture Using Simple Shapes

Here is a group of buildings painted in a **style** similar to the pictures on pages 14 and 15. Look at how the artist has used blocks of color to make the simple shapes of the buildings stronger. The **rectangular** shapes of the houses and their roofs give the picture its **solid** feel. The artist has used little **detail**, but the painting comes alive.

André Derain, *At La Roche Guillon*, 1910

Copy one of these buildings carefully. Color it in using blocks of **earth colors**—brown, yellow, and red. Now put tree shapes in the background. Add other shapes until you have made a complete **scene**.

Using Everyday Objects

Samuel John Peploe,
Still Life, about 1913

A picture of everyday objects is called a still life. Many artists enjoy painting this kind of picture because they can make ordinary things look special. Here the shapes and colors of the background are **repeated** in the objects themselves. This repetition makes it difficult to see where one object ends and another begins.

Take three or four simple objects and arrange them in a way that interests you. Draw them as best you can. You may want to try this a few times to get the best view. Now draw lines across and down the page to divide the background space, as shown in the example. Color the shapes and background so the objects really stand out.

27

Make a Picture Book

Some of the earliest books were made in China using the method shown below. Books made this way are called **concertina books**.

1. Fold a piece of paper into eight rectangles.
2. Open the paper out and fold it again on the longest line.
3. Fold it in half, then fold one end towards you and the other away from you.
4. Number the pages. Put 1 on the cover, and then 2 to 8 for the rest.

Choose some shapes and make your own **abstract** picture on the first page of your concertina book. Think about how the shapes fit together. **Repeat** the picture on the other pages of the book, but move the shapes around and change their colors and size. Finally, think of a good title for the cover.

Glossary

abstract kind of art that does not try to show people or things, but instead focuses on shape and color

bronze hard, shiny metal made from copper and tin used in sculpture

concertina book book that folds up like an accordion

contrast to show a noticeable difference

Cubism style of painting that uses simple shapes and shows each object from different angles or viewpoints in the same picture

detail small part of a picture; part of a picture that adds to its meaning

earth color warm color found in nature, such as brown or red

emotion strong feeling

emphasize to draw special attention to something

grief terrible sadness

landscape picture of outdoor scenery, such as fields, trees, and houses

marble type of stone that many artists use for sculpture because it can be highly polished

mosaic picture or pattern made with small colored stones, tiles, or pieces of glass

outline line that shows the edge and shape of an object

portrait painting or photograph of a person

rectangular in the shape of a rectangle

repeat to do something over and over again

scene view painted by an artist or place where something happens

sculpture three-dimensional art made with wood, clay, stone, or metal

shade darker or lighter version of a color

solid looking like a real, physical object; having a defined form and weight

style way that a picture is painted

triangular in the shape of a triangle

More Books to Read

Cush, Cathie. *Artists Who Created Great Works.* Austin, Tex.: Raintree Steck-Vaughn, 1994.

Richardson, Joy. *Using Shadows in Art.* Milwaukee, Wisc.: Gareth Stevens, 1999.

Steele, Margaret, and Cindy Estes. *The Art of Shapes: For Children and Adults.* Los Angeles: The Museum of Contemporary Art, 1997.

Index